advertising to re-engage customers who have shown interest in your product or similar items.

For authors, Sponsored Products are the most commonly used ad type, as they directly promote a book to potential readers based on specific search terms.

The Role of Keywords in Amazon Sponsored Ads

Keywords are the foundation of any successful Amazon ad campaign. They act as the link between what customers are searching for and the products or books you're advertising. When a shopper enters a search term into Amazon's search bar, the platform uses its algorithm to match that query with relevant ads based on the keywords you've chosen.

Here's why keywords matter:
- Visibility: The right keywords ensure your ad appears in front of the right audience. If your keywords match what shoppers are searching for, your ad is more likely to be displayed.
- Relevance: Keywords help Amazon determine how closely your product matches customer intent. Relevant keywords lead to higher click-through rates (CTR) and conversions.
- Cost Efficiency: By targeting specific keywords, you can avoid wasting money on irrelevant clicks from shoppers who aren't interested in your product.

How Amazon Matches Ads with Keywords

Amazon uses an auction-based system to determine which ads appear for a given search query. Here's how it works:
1. When a shopper searches for something (e.g., "mystery thriller book"), Amazon scans all active ad campaigns with keywords that match or relate to that query.
2. Advertisers bid on these keywords, setting a maximum amount they're willing to pay per click (CPC).
3. The algorithm considers both the bid amount and the ad's relevance (based on factors like keyword match type and product performance) to decide which ads to display and in what order.

The better your keyword targeting and ad relevance, the more likely your ad will win placements—even if your bid isn't the highest.

Keyword Match Types: Broad, Phrase, and Exact

Amazon allows advertisers to choose from three keyword match types, each offering different levels of control over when an ad appears:

1. Broad Match:
   - Your ad may show up for searches that include your keyword in any order, along with related terms.
   - Example: If your keyword is "mystery thriller," your ad could appear for searches like

"thriller mystery," "best mystery books," or "thriller novels."
   - Best for: Reaching a wider audience and discovering new keyword opportunities.

2. Phrase Match:
   - Your ad will only appear if the shopper's query includes your exact keyword phrase in the correct order, though other words can appear before or after it.
   - Example: For "mystery thriller," your ad might show up for "best mystery thriller books" but not "thriller books mystery."
   - Best for: Targeting more specific searches while maintaining some flexibility.

3. Exact Match:
   - Your ad will only show up if the shopper's query matches your keyword exactly (or is a close variation).
   - Example: For "mystery thriller," your ad would only display for searches like "mystery thriller" or "mystery thrillers."
   - Best for: Precise targeting with higher conversion potential.

Choosing the right mix of match types is crucial for balancing reach and relevance in your campaigns.

The Importance of Relevance

Amazon prioritizes customer experience above all else. This means that even if you bid high on a keyword, your ad won't perform well unless it's relevant to what shoppers are searching for. To ensure relevance:
- Use keywords that accurately describe your book or product.
- Avoid overly broad terms that could lead to irrelevant clicks (e.g., using "fiction" instead of "historical fiction").
- Continuously monitor performance and refine your keyword list based on what resonates with shoppers.

Key Metrics to Monitor

To evaluate the success of your campaigns, keep an eye on these key metrics:
- Click-Through Rate (CTR): The percentage of people who click on your ad after seeing it. A high CTR indicates that your keywords are attracting relevant traffic.
- Conversion Rate: The percentage of clicks that result in a sale. This shows how effective your keywords are at driving purchases.
- Advertising Cost of Sales (ACoS): The ratio of ad spend to sales revenue generated by ads. A lower ACoS means better profitability.

Understanding these metrics will help you optimize your campaigns over time and ensure you're getting the most out of your keyword strategy.

Conclusion

Keywords for Amazon Sponsored Ads: A Comprehensive Guide to Boosting Visibility and Sales

Copyright © 2024-2025 ROIAble Publishing.
All rights reserved. No part of this book may be reproduced, distributed, or transmitted in any form or by any means, including photocopying, recording, or other electronic or mechanical methods.

Earnings and Results Disclaimer

The strategies, techniques, and examples provided in this book, "Keywords for Amazon Sponsored Ads: A Comprehensive Guide to Boosting Visibility and Sales," are intended for informational and educational purposes only. While every effort has been made to ensure the accuracy and effectiveness of the content, the results you achieve may vary based on numerous factors, including but not limited to your product category, competition, budget, experience level, and market conditions.

No Guaranteed Results
This book does not guarantee specific results such as increased sales, reduced advertising costs, or improved campaign performance. Success with Amazon Sponsored Ads depends on individual implementation, continuous monitoring, and adjustments based on data. The case studies and examples provided are illustrative and may not reflect typical outcomes.

Earnings Disclaimer
Any references to earnings or financial performance in this book are for illustrative purposes only. They are not guarantees of future income or success. Your actual earnings will depend on various factors unique to your business, including the quality of your product or book, your advertising strategy, market demand, and customer behavior. Advertising carries inherent risks, and there is no assurance that you will achieve profitability.

Responsibility
Readers are solely responsible for their decisions and actions based on the information provided in this book. The author and publisher disclaim any liability for losses or damages incurred as a result of applying the strategies discussed herein.

Professional Advice
This book is not a substitute for professional advice. If you require legal, financial, or business advice specific to your situation, consult with qualified professionals before making decisions related to advertising or business operations.

By using the information in this book, you acknowledge that the author and publisher are not responsible for your success or failure as a result of implementing these strategies. Your results will depend on your effort, commitment, and ability to adapt to changing market conditions.

Introduction

In the competitive world of e-commerce, standing out on Amazon is no small feat. With millions of products vying for attention, authors, sellers, and brands must find effective ways to connect with their target audience. One of the most powerful tools at your disposal is Amazon Sponsored Ads, a pay-per-click (PPC) advertising platform that allows you to promote your products directly to potential buyers. At the heart of every successful Amazon ad campaign lies a well-researched and strategically implemented keyword strategy.

Keywords are the bridge between what customers are searching for and what you're offering. They determine whether your product appears in search results, how relevant it is to customer queries, and, ultimately, whether shoppers click on your ad. For authors and sellers alike, understanding how to select and use keywords effectively can mean the difference between a high-performing campaign and wasted ad spend.

This book is designed to demystify the process of using keywords in Amazon Sponsored Ads. Whether you're an author promoting your latest book or a seller looking to boost product visibility, this guide will walk you through everything you need to know—from understanding keyword types and researching effective terms to optimizing your campaigns for maximum return on investment.

You'll learn:
- How Amazon's advertising system works and why keywords are critical.
- The different types of keywords (broad match, phrase match, exact match) and when to use them.
- How to build a keyword strategy tailored to your product or book.
- Advanced techniques for discovering high-converting keywords.
- Tips for managing budgets, reducing wasted spend with negative keywords, and refining campaigns over time.

By the end of this book, you'll have a clear roadmap for creating keyword-driven ad campaigns that not only drive traffic but also convert clicks into sales. Whether you're new to Amazon advertising or looking to refine your existing strategy, this guide will equip you with the knowledge and tools needed to succeed.

Let's dive in and unlock the power of keywords for Amazon Sponsored Ads!

Chapter 1: Understanding Amazon Sponsored Ads

Amazon is not just the world's largest online marketplace—it's also a powerful search engine where millions of customers actively look for products they want to buy. Unlike traditional advertising platforms, Amazon's Sponsored Ads are designed to connect sellers and authors directly with shoppers who are already in the buying mindset. To succeed in this environment, it's essential to understand how Amazon Sponsored Ads work and the critical role that keywords play in driving visibility and sales.

What Are Amazon Sponsored Ads?

Amazon Sponsored Ads are a type of pay-per-click (PPC) advertising that allows sellers, authors, and brands to promote their products or books on Amazon. These ads appear in prominent locations, such as:
- The top of search results pages.
- Product detail pages.
- Alongside related product recommendations.

There are three main types of Amazon Sponsored Ads:
1. Sponsored Products: These ads promote individual products or books and appear in search results or on product detail pages. They are ideal for driving traffic to a specific item.
2. Sponsored Brands: These ads showcase a brand logo, a custom headline, and multiple products. They are useful for building brand awareness and promoting a portfolio of products.
3. Sponsored Display: These ads target shoppers both on and off Amazon, using display

Amazon Sponsored Ads offer unparalleled opportunities to reach customers who are actively searching for products like yours—but success hinges on mastering keywords. By understanding how Amazon's advertising system works and leveraging different match types strategically, you can create campaigns that drive visibility, clicks, and conversions. In the next chapter, we'll dive deeper into the different types of keywords you can use and how to choose them effectively for maximum impact.

Chapter 2: Types of Keywords for Amazon Ads

Keywords are the backbone of Amazon Sponsored Ads. They determine how, when, and where your ads appear in search results, making them critical to the success of your campaigns. However, not all keywords are created equal. Understanding the different types of keywords and how to use them effectively is essential for crafting a winning strategy.

In this chapter, we'll explore the various types of keywords you can use in Amazon ads, their unique purposes, and how to choose the right ones for your campaigns.

1. Broad Match Keywords

Broad match keywords are the most flexible type of keyword targeting in Amazon ads. When you use a broad match keyword, your ad can appear for searches that include your keyword in any order, as well as related terms and synonyms.

- **Example:** If your broad match keyword is "self-help book," your ad might show up for:
  - "best self-help books"
  - "books for personal growth"
  - "self improvement book"

- **Advantages:**
  - Broad match keywords allow you to reach a wide audience.
  - They are useful for discovering new search terms that customers are using to find products like yours.
  - They can help you identify trends or unexpected keywords that resonate with shoppers.

- **Disadvantages:**
  - The flexibility of broad match targeting can lead to irrelevant clicks if your ad appears for unrelated searches.
  - This can result in wasted ad spend if not monitored carefully.

- **When to Use:**
  - Broad match keywords are ideal for the initial stages of a campaign when you're trying to gather data and explore which terms generate interest.

2. Phrase Match Keywords

Phrase match keywords offer more control than broad match by requiring that your keyword phrase appears in the customer's search query in the exact order you specify. However, additional words can be included before or after the phrase.

- Example: If your phrase match keyword is "self-help book," your ad might show up for:
  - "best self-help book for women"
  - "self-help book recommendations"

But it will not appear for:
- "books about self improvement"
- "helpful books on growth"

- Advantages:
  - Phrase match keywords strike a balance between reach and relevance.
  - They ensure your ad is shown to shoppers with specific intent while still allowing some flexibility.

- Disadvantages:
  - While more targeted than broad match, phrase match still risks appearing for searches that aren't fully aligned with your product (e.g., overly generic queries).

- When to Use:
  - Use phrase match keywords when you want to target slightly refined audiences who are searching for terms closely related to your product or book.

3. Exact Match Keywords

Exact match keywords provide the highest level of precision in targeting. Your ad will only appear when a customer's search query matches your keyword exactly (or is a close variation). This includes singular/plural forms or minor misspellings but excludes additional words.

- Example: If your exact match keyword is "self-help book," your ad might show up for:
  - "self-help book"
  - "self help books"

But it will not appear for:
- "best self-help book"
- "books about self-help"

- Advantages:
  - Exact match keywords offer maximum control over when and where your ads appear.
  - They typically result in higher click-through rates (CTR) and conversion rates because

they align perfectly with customer intent.
 - They help minimize wasted ad spend by avoiding irrelevant clicks.

- Disadvantages:
 - The narrow scope of exact match targeting limits reach.
 - You may miss out on potential customers who use variations or related terms in their searches.

- When to Use:
 - Use exact match keywords when you have a clear understanding of high-performing search terms and want to focus on driving conversions efficiently.

4. Long-Tail Keywords

Long-tail keywords are highly specific phrases that often include three or more words. These keywords tend to have lower search volume but higher conversion potential because they reflect precise customer intent.

- Example: Instead of using a general keyword like "self-help," a long-tail keyword might be "self-help book for anxiety."

- Advantages:
 - Long-tail keywords face less competition compared to shorter, more generic terms.
 - They attract highly targeted traffic, leading to better conversion rates.

- Disadvantages:
 - Lower search volume means fewer impressions overall.

- When to Use:
 - Long-tail keywords are best suited for niche products or books where specificity is key to attracting the right audience.

5. Branded Keywords

Branded keywords include the name of an author, brand, or product. These keywords are particularly useful for protecting your brand identity and ensuring that customers searching specifically for you find your products first.

- Example: If you're an author named Jane Doe, branded keywords might include:
 - "Jane Doe books"
 - "Jane Doe self-help"

- Advantages:
 - Branded keywords capture customers who already know about you or your product.
 - They prevent competitors from stealing traffic by bidding on your brand name.

- Disadvantages:

- Branded keywords may not attract new customers since they target those already familiar with your brand.

- When to Use:
  - Use branded keywords as part of a defensive strategy to protect your market share and ensure visibility among loyal customers.

6. Competitor Keywords

Competitor keywords involve targeting the names of competing brands, authors, or products. This strategy can help you attract shoppers who are considering alternatives but haven't made a final decision yet.

- Example: If another author writes similar books in the self-help genre, you might bid on their name as a keyword (e.g., "John Smith self-help books").

- Advantages:
  - Competitor keywords allow you to capture traffic from shoppers who are already interested in similar products.

- Disadvantages:
  - Bidding on competitor names can be expensive due to high competition.
  - It may lead to lower conversion rates if shoppers are loyal to the competitor's brand.

- When to Use:
  - Use competitor keywords strategically when you offer clear advantages over competitors (e.g., better reviews, lower prices).

Choosing the Right Mix of Keywords

A successful campaign often combines multiple types of keywords. Here's how you can approach it:

1. Start with broad match and phrase match keywords during initial campaigns to gather data on search terms that resonate with shoppers.
2. Gradually refine your list by identifying high-performing search terms and transitioning them into exact match or long-tail keywords.
3. Incorporate branded and competitor keywords strategically based on your goals (e.g., building awareness vs. defending market share).
4. Continuously monitor performance metrics like click-through rate (CTR), conversion rate, and advertising cost of sales (ACoS) to optimize your keyword mix over time.

Conclusion

Understanding the different types of keywords is critical for building an effective Amazon

Sponsored Ads strategy. Each type serves a unique purpose—broad match helps you cast a wide net, phrase match balances reach with relevance, and exact match targets highly specific queries with precision. By combining these with long-tail, branded, and competitor-focused strategies, you can create campaigns that maximize visibility while driving meaningful conversions. In the next chapter, we'll dive into how to build an effective keyword strategy tailored specifically to your product or book.

Chapter 3: Building an Effective Keyword Strategy

Crafting a strong keyword strategy is the cornerstone of a successful Amazon Sponsored Ads campaign. A well-thought-out strategy ensures your ads appear in front of the right audience, maximizing visibility, clicks, and conversions while minimizing wasted ad spend. In this chapter, we'll explore how to create a keyword strategy tailored to your product or book, using both data-driven techniques and creative approaches.

1. Start with Automatic Campaigns for Discovery

If you're new to Amazon advertising or unsure which keywords will perform best, automatic campaigns are a great starting point. In an automatic campaign, Amazon's algorithm determines which search terms trigger your ads based on your product's metadata (title, description, etc.).

- Benefits:
  - Automatic campaigns help identify high-performing keywords that you might not have considered.
  - They provide valuable data through the Search Term Report, showing which terms generate impressions, clicks, and conversions.

- How to Use Automatic Campaigns:
  - Run an automatic campaign for at least two weeks to gather sufficient data.
  - Review the Search Term Report to identify keywords that drive sales or generate significant interest.
  - Transfer successful keywords from automatic campaigns into manual campaigns for more precise targeting and control.

2. Transition to Manual Campaigns

Once you've identified effective keywords from your automatic campaign, it's time to set up manual campaigns. Manual campaigns allow you to choose specific keywords and match types (broad, phrase, or exact) for targeted advertising.

- Steps for Manual Campaigns:
  1. Create separate ad groups for broad, phrase, and exact match keywords.
  2. Use broad match keywords for discovery and reach.
  3. Use phrase match keywords for moderately refined targeting.
  4. Use exact match keywords for precise targeting with high conversion potential.

- Tip: Start with a mix of keyword match types and monitor performance over time. Adjust bids based on the keywords' effectiveness.

3. Identify High-Performing Keywords

High-performing keywords are those that consistently generate clicks and conversions at a reasonable cost-per-click (CPC). These are often referred to as positive keywords.

- How to Identify High-Performing Keywords:
    - Use the Search Term Report from your campaigns to find terms with high click-through rates (CTR) and conversion rates.
    - Focus on buyer-intent keywords—terms that reflect a customer's readiness to purchase (e.g., "best self-help book for anxiety" rather than just "self-help book").
    - Consider long-tail keywords with lower competition but higher specificity.

- What to Do with High-Performing Keywords:
    - Increase bids on these keywords in manual campaigns to improve their visibility.
    - Use them as the foundation of exact match campaigns for maximum efficiency.

4. Incorporate Branded and Competitor Keywords

Branded and competitor keywords can play a strategic role in your keyword strategy:

- Branded Keywords:
    - Include your brand name or product name as keywords (e.g., "Jane Doe books").
    - These ensure that customers searching specifically for you can easily find your products.
    - Safely bid higher on branded keywords since they often have high conversion rates.

- Competitor Keywords:
    - Target competitor brand names or product names (e.g., "John Smith self-help books").
    - This can help capture traffic from shoppers considering alternatives.
    - Monitor performance closely, as competitor keywords may have lower conversion rates or higher CPCs due to competition.

5. Refine Your Keyword List with Negative Keywords

Negative keywords are terms you exclude from your campaigns to prevent your ads from appearing in irrelevant searches. This helps reduce wasted ad spend and improves overall campaign efficiency.

- How to Identify Negative Keywords:
    - Look for search terms in the Search Term Report that generate clicks but no conversions.
    - Exclude overly broad terms that attract irrelevant traffic (e.g., "free self-help books").

- Examples of Negative Keywords:
  - If you're selling premium products, exclude terms like "cheap" or "discount."
  - If you're targeting adult readers, exclude terms like "children's books."

6. Leverage Seasonal and Trending Keywords

Seasonal and trending keywords can boost sales during specific times of the year or in response to market trends.

- Seasonal Keywords:
  - Add holiday-related terms during peak seasons (e.g., "Mother's Day gifts" or "Christmas self-help books").

- Trending Keywords:
  - Monitor current events or cultural trends that may influence customer searches.

- Tip: Seasonal and trending keywords often have fluctuating performance. Monitor them closely and adjust bids as needed.

7. Organize Keywords by Relevance

Grouping similar keywords into ad groups ensures better organization and relevance within your campaigns:

- Create ad groups based on themes like product features, benefits, or audience demographics.
- For example:
  - Group A: Keywords related to anxiety relief (e.g., "self-help book for anxiety").
  - Group B: Keywords targeting productivity improvement (e.g., "time management book").

This structure improves ad relevance scores and helps Amazon's algorithm better match your ads with customer searches.

8. Monitor Performance Metrics Regularly

Keyword performance is dynamic; what works today may not work tomorrow due to changing customer behavior or increased competition.

- Key metrics to track include:
  - Impressions: How often your ad is shown.
  - Click-Through Rate (CTR): The percentage of impressions that result in clicks.
  - Conversion Rate: The percentage of clicks that result in sales.
  - Advertising Cost of Sales (ACoS): The ratio of ad spend to sales revenue generated by ads.

Use these metrics to refine your keyword strategy by increasing bids on high-performing terms and reducing bids on underperforming ones.

9. Experiment with Bid Adjustments

Your bidding strategy directly impacts the visibility of your ads:

- Bid higher on exact match and high-converting keywords to secure top placements.
- Lower bids on broad match keywords since they tend to have lower conversion rates but broader reach.
- Test different bid amounts over time to find the optimal balance between cost-efficiency and visibility.

10. Continuously Harvest New Keywords

Keyword harvesting is an ongoing process where you identify new profitable search terms:

- Use data from ongoing campaigns (especially broad match) to discover new opportunities.
- Regularly update your keyword list based on emerging trends or shifts in customer behavior.

Conclusion

Building an effective keyword strategy requires a combination of research, experimentation, and ongoing optimization. By starting with automatic campaigns, transitioning into manual targeting, identifying high-performing terms, leveraging branded/competitor/seasonal keywords, and refining with negative terms, you can create a robust system that drives visibility and sales while minimizing wasted spend. In the next chapter, we'll delve into advanced techniques like keyword harvesting and bid optimization to take your campaigns to the next level!

Chapter 4: Advanced Keyword Research Techniques

Keyword research is not a one-time task; it's an ongoing process that requires refinement, analysis, and adaptation to stay competitive in Amazon's ever-evolving marketplace. While basic strategies like using Amazon's autocomplete or targeting obvious keywords can yield results, advanced techniques can uncover untapped opportunities that many competitors overlook. In this chapter, we'll explore advanced methods for conducting keyword research and how to implement these findings to maximize the effectiveness of your Amazon Sponsored Ads.

1. Reverse ASIN Lookup

One of the most powerful tools in advanced keyword research is the reverse ASIN lookup. This technique allows you to analyze your competitors' product listings to identify the keywords they are ranking for.

- How It Works:
  - Input a competitor's ASIN (Amazon Standard Identification Number) into a reverse ASIN tool (e.g., Helium 10's Cerebro or AMZScout).
  - The tool generates a list of keywords driving traffic to that product, along with data such as search volume, competition level, and estimated cost-per-click (CPC).

- Benefits:
  - Discover high-performing keywords that your competitors are targeting.
  - Identify gaps in your own keyword strategy by comparing it with competitors.
  - Gain insights into niche or long-tail keywords with lower competition.

- Implementation:
  - Use the keywords you uncover to refine your campaigns by targeting terms that are both relevant and less saturated.

2. Long-Tail Keyword Targeting

Long-tail keywords are highly specific phrases that often include three or more words. While they may have lower search volumes than broader terms, they tend to attract shoppers with strong purchase intent, resulting in higher conversion rates.

- Examples:
  - Instead of targeting a broad term like "self-help book," use long-tail variations like "self-help book for anxiety" or "self-help book for time management."

- How to Find Long-Tail Keywords:
  - Use Amazon's autocomplete feature by typing in a core keyword and noting the suggestions.
  - Employ tools like Jungle Scout's Keyword Scout or Helium 10's Magnet to generate long-tail keyword ideas.
  - Analyze customer reviews and questions on similar products to identify commonly used phrases.

- Why It Works:
  - Long-tail keywords face less competition, making them more cost-effective for PPC campaigns.
  - They align closely with customer intent, improving click-through rates (CTR) and conversions.

3. Competitor Analysis

Studying your competitors is an essential part of advanced keyword research. By analyzing their strategies, you can identify opportunities to outperform them.

- Steps for Competitor Analysis:
  1. Identify top-performing competitors in your niche.
  2. Use reverse ASIN tools or manual analysis to uncover their targeted keywords.
  3. Evaluate their product titles, descriptions, and bullet points for additional keyword ideas.

- Key Insights to Look For:
  - Which keywords are driving sales for competitors?
  - Are there any trending or seasonal keywords they're targeting?
  - What gaps exist in their strategy that you can capitalize on?

- Pro Tip: Combine competitor data with your own campaign metrics to refine your keyword list further.

4. Using Amazon Search Term Reports

If you're already running Amazon ads, your existing campaign data is a goldmine for discovering high-potential keywords. The Search Term Report provides detailed insights into the actual search terms customers used before clicking on your ad.

- How to Use Search Term Reports:
  - Identify search terms with high CTRs and conversion rates.
  - Add these terms as exact match or phrase match keywords in manual campaigns.
  - Exclude irrelevant or low-performing terms by adding them as negative keywords.

- Benefits:
  - Real-world data ensures you're targeting terms that resonate with customers.
  - Helps refine your campaigns for better efficiency and ROI.

5. Seasonal and Trending Keywords

Seasonality and trends play a significant role in customer search behavior on Amazon. Incorporating seasonal or trending keywords into your campaigns can help capture demand spikes during specific times of the year or in response to cultural events.

- Examples of Seasonal Keywords:
  - During the holiday season: "Christmas gift books" or "holiday self-help guides."
  - Around back-to-school time: "self-help books for students."

- How to Identify Trends:
  - Use tools like Google Trends or Helium 10's Trendster to track keyword popularity over

time.
- Monitor social media platforms and industry news for emerging topics relevant to your niche.

- Implementation:
  - Create separate ad groups for seasonal/trending keywords.
  - Adjust bids based on demand fluctuations during peak periods.

6. Categorizing Keywords

Organizing your keywords into categories helps streamline campaign management and ensures better targeting. Consider segmenting your keywords into three main groups:

1. Golden Keywords: High-relevance, high-volume terms that drive significant traffic (e.g., "self-help books").
2. Efficiency Keywords: Moderate-volume terms with strong conversion potential (e.g., "self-help book for anxiety").
3. Related Keywords: Broader or complementary terms that may attract secondary audiences (e.g., "personal growth books").

By categorizing keywords, you can allocate budgets more effectively and tailor ad copy to specific audience segments.

7. Advanced Tools for Keyword Research

Several third-party tools provide advanced features for uncovering profitable keywords:

- Helium 10 Cerebro:
  - Conduct reverse ASIN lookups.
  - Filter results by search volume, competition level, and relevancy.

- Jungle Scout Keyword Scout:
  - Generate thousands of relevant keywords instantly.
  - Access metrics like estimated PPC costs and competition levels.

- AMZScout Reverse ASIN Lookup:
  - Analyze competitor performance and discover untapped keyword opportunities.

These tools save time while providing actionable insights tailored specifically for Amazon PPC campaigns.

8. Refining Your Keyword Strategy Over Time

Keyword research is not static; it requires constant refinement based on performance data and market trends.

- Regularly review campaign metrics like CTR, conversion rate, and ACoS (Advertising Cost of Sales).
- Update your keyword list by adding new high-performing terms and removing underperforming ones.
- Revisit competitor strategies periodically to stay ahead in the marketplace.

By continuously optimizing your keyword strategy, you ensure long-term success in driving visibility and sales on Amazon.

Conclusion

Advanced keyword research techniques like reverse ASIN lookups, long-tail targeting, competitor analysis, and leveraging search term reports can unlock new opportunities that basic strategies often miss. By combining these methods with tools like Helium 10 or Jungle Scout—and refining your approach over time—you can stay ahead of the competition while maximizing the effectiveness of your Amazon Sponsored Ads campaigns. In the next chapter, we'll delve into creating compelling ad copy that converts clicks into sales!

Chapter 5: Negative Keywords and Budget Optimization

Running a successful Amazon Sponsored Ads campaign isn't just about finding the right keywords—it's also about avoiding the wrong ones. Negative keywords are a powerful tool that can help you refine your ad targeting, reduce wasted ad spend, and improve overall campaign performance. In this chapter, we'll explore how to use negative keywords effectively and how to optimize your budget for maximum return on investment (ROI).

1. What Are Negative Keywords?

Negative keywords are terms that you specifically exclude from your ad campaigns. By adding negative keywords, you prevent your ads from appearing in search results for queries that are irrelevant to your product or unlikely to convert into sales.

- Example:
  - If you're advertising a premium self-help book, you might add "free" or "cheap" as negative keywords to avoid clicks from shoppers looking for low-cost or free options.

- Why Negative Keywords Matter:
  - They eliminate irrelevant traffic, ensuring your ads are only shown to potential customers who are more likely to purchase.
  - They help reduce wasted ad spend by preventing clicks on unqualified leads.

- They improve your campaign's overall performance metrics, such as click-through rate (CTR) and conversion rate.

2. Types of Negative Keywords

Amazon allows you to add negative keywords in two match types:

1. Negative Phrase Match:
    - Your ad will not appear if the search query contains the exact phrase in the specified order.
    - Example: If "free self-help book" is a negative phrase match, your ad won't show for "best free self-help book," but it may still appear for "free books about self-help."

2. Negative Exact Match:
    - Your ad will not appear if the search query matches the keyword exactly.
    - Example: If "self-help book free" is a negative exact match, your ad won't show for that exact query but could still appear for "self-help book free download."

- When to Use Each Type:
    - Use negative phrase match for broader exclusions (e.g., "cheap books").
    - Use negative exact match for highly specific exclusions (e.g., "self-help book free PDF").

3. How to Identify Negative Keywords

To identify which terms should be added as negative keywords, analyze your campaign data and customer behavior:

- Search Term Reports:
    - Review Amazon's Search Term Report to find queries that generate clicks but no conversions.
    - Look for patterns in irrelevant searches (e.g., terms like "free," "used," or unrelated topics).

- Common Irrelevant Terms:
    - Generic terms that don't align with your product (e.g., if you're selling a niche book, exclude terms like "fiction" or "general books").
    - Misleading terms (e.g., if your book is digital-only, exclude terms like "paperback" or "hardcover").

- Customer Feedback:
    - Monitor customer reviews and questions on your product page for clues about potential misunderstandings or mismatches in expectations.

4. Examples of Negative Keywords

Here are some examples of negative keywords based on different scenarios:

- For a premium product:
  - Negative keywords: "cheap," "discount," "bargain"

- For a digital-only product:
  - Negative keywords: "paperback," "hardcover," "physical copy"

- For targeting adult readers:
  - Negative keywords: "children's books," "kids"

By tailoring negative keywords to your specific product or audience, you can ensure your ads are reaching the right shoppers.

5. Implementing Negative Keywords in Campaigns

Adding negative keywords to your campaigns is simple but requires strategic placement:

1. At the Campaign Level:
   - Apply negative keywords at the campaign level if they are universally irrelevant across all ad groups within the campaign.

2. At the Ad Group Level:
   - Apply negative keywords at the ad group level if they are only irrelevant to specific product categories or audiences.

3. Regular Updates:
   - Continuously update your negative keyword list based on new data from Search Term Reports and campaign performance.

6. Budget Optimization Strategies

In addition to refining targeting with negative keywords, optimizing your budget is crucial for maximizing ROI. Here's how to allocate and manage your budget effectively:

- Set Realistic Daily Budgets:
  - Start with a daily budget that aligns with your overall advertising goals and financial capacity.
  - Monitor performance and adjust budgets based on which campaigns deliver the best results.

- Prioritize High-Converting Keywords:
  - Allocate more budget to campaigns or ad groups featuring high-performing keywords.

- Reduce spend on underperforming campaigns by lowering bids or pausing low-converting keywords.

- **Use Bid Adjustments Strategically:**
  - Increase bids on exact match and high-converting long-tail keywords to secure better placements.
  - Lower bids on broad match keywords that generate impressions but few conversions.

- **Leverage Dayparting (if applicable):**
  - Analyze when your target audience is most active and adjust bids or budgets accordingly.
  - For example, if most sales occur in the evening, allocate more budget during those hours.

- **Monitor ACoS (Advertising Cost of Sales):**
  - Track ACoS regularly to ensure profitability.
  - Aim for an ACoS that aligns with your profit margins—lower ACoS means better returns on ad spend.

7. Common Budget Optimization Mistakes to Avoid

While optimizing budgets can significantly improve campaign performance, there are common pitfalls to watch out for:

- **Overbidding on Broad Match Keywords:**
  - Broad match keywords can drain budgets quickly without delivering conversions. Keep bids conservative unless they prove effective.

- **Ignoring Low-Impression Keywords:**
  - Don't immediately discard low-impression keywords; instead, analyze their relevance and consider adjusting bids or using them in long-tail variations.

- **Failing to Reallocate Budgets Regularly:**
  - Campaign performance changes over time due to seasonality, competition, and customer behavior. Regularly review and reallocate budgets based on current data.

8. Tools for Managing Negative Keywords and Budgets

Several tools can help streamline keyword management and budget optimization:

- **Amazon Advertising Console:**
  - Provides built-in features for adding negative keywords and monitoring campaign performance.

- **Third-Party Tools:**
  - Tools like Helium 10, Sellics, or Jungle Scout offer advanced features for automating keyword management and tracking ROI.

9. The Impact of Negative Keywords on Campaign Performance

Using negative keywords effectively can have a significant impact on key performance metrics:

- **Improved CTR:** By eliminating irrelevant impressions, you increase the likelihood of attracting qualified clicks.
- **Higher Conversion Rates:** Targeting only relevant audiences leads to more purchases.
- **Lower ACoS:** Reducing wasted spend improves profitability by ensuring every dollar is spent efficiently.

Conclusion

Negative keywords are an essential component of any Amazon Sponsored Ads strategy. By excluding irrelevant terms and optimizing budgets strategically, you can refine your campaigns to target only high-potential customers while minimizing wasted spend. Combined with ongoing analysis and adjustments, these techniques will help you achieve better results while maintaining cost efficiency. In the next chapter, we'll explore how to monitor campaign performance effectively and make data-driven adjustments for continuous improvement!

Chapter 6: Monitoring and Adjusting Campaigns

Creating a successful Amazon Sponsored Ads campaign doesn't stop at launching it. To achieve long-term success, you need to continuously monitor performance and make data-driven adjustments. Amazon's advertising platform provides a wealth of insights that can help you refine your strategy, optimize ad spend, and improve key metrics like click-through rate (CTR), conversion rate, and Advertising Cost of Sales (ACoS). In this chapter, we'll explore how to evaluate campaign performance and implement changes to maximize results.

1. Why Monitoring Campaigns Is Essential

Monitoring your campaigns regularly allows you to:
- Identify high-performing keywords and ad groups.
- Spot underperforming elements that need adjustment or removal.
- Ensure your ad spend is aligned with your goals.
- Adapt to market changes, such as seasonal trends or increased competition.

Without consistent monitoring, you risk wasting money on ineffective ads or missing opportunities to capitalize on successful ones.

2. Key Metrics to Track

To evaluate the effectiveness of your campaigns, focus on these essential metrics:

- **Impressions:**
  - The number of times your ad is shown to customers.
  - High impressions with low clicks may indicate irrelevant targeting or weak ad copy.

- **Click-Through Rate (CTR):**
  - The percentage of impressions that result in clicks.
  - Formula: $$\text{CTR} = \frac{\text{Clicks}}{\text{Impressions}} \times 100$$
  - A low CTR suggests that your ad isn't resonating with customers—this could be due to poor keyword selection, irrelevant targeting, or unappealing ad content.

- **Conversion Rate:**
  - The percentage of clicks that result in a sale.
  - Formula: $$\text{Conversion Rate} = \frac{\text{Orders}}{\text{Clicks}} \times 100$$
  - A low conversion rate may indicate issues with your product listing (e.g., pricing, reviews, or product images).

- **Advertising Cost of Sales (ACoS):**
  - The ratio of ad spend to sales revenue generated by ads.
  - Formula: $$\text{ACoS} = \frac{\text{Ad Spend}}{\text{Ad Revenue}} \times 100$$
  - A lower ACoS indicates better profitability. Aim for an ACoS that aligns with your profit margins.

- **Return on Ad Spend (ROAS):**
  - The inverse of ACoS; it measures how much revenue you earn for every dollar spent on ads.
  - Formula: $$\text{ROAS} = \frac{\text{Ad Revenue}}{\text{Ad Spend}}$$

By tracking these metrics, you can identify what's working and what needs improvement.

3. Analyzing Campaign Performance

Amazon provides several tools for analyzing campaign performance:

- Campaign Dashboard:
  - Offers an overview of impressions, clicks, CTR, sales, and ACoS for each campaign.
  - Use this dashboard to compare the performance of different campaigns at a glance.

- Search Term Report:
  - Shows the exact search terms customers used before clicking on your ad.
  - Use this report to identify high-performing keywords and irrelevant terms that should be added as negative keywords.

- Placement Reports:

- Provide insights into where your ads are showing (e.g., top of search results vs. product pages).
- Adjust bids based on placement performance—for example, increase bids for placements that drive more conversions.

- Performance Over Time:
  - Analyze trends in performance metrics over time to identify patterns or seasonal fluctuations.

4. Adjusting Bids Based on Performance

Bid adjustments are one of the most effective ways to optimize your campaigns. Here's how to approach it:

- Increase Bids for High-Converting Keywords:
  - If a keyword consistently drives sales at a profitable ACoS, consider increasing its bid to improve visibility and capture more traffic.

- Lower Bids for Low-Converting Keywords:
  - For keywords with high clicks but few conversions, reduce bids to minimize wasted spend.

- Pause Non-Performing Keywords:
  - If a keyword generates significant impressions or clicks without any sales over time, consider pausing it altogether.

- Adjust Placement-Specific Bids:
  - Use Amazon's placement reports to identify which placements perform best (e.g., top of search). Increase placement-specific bids for high-performing locations.

5. Refining Keyword Targeting

As you gather more data from your campaigns, refine your keyword strategy:

- Promote High-Performing Keywords:
  - Move high-converting keywords into exact match campaigns for more precise targeting.

- Discover New Opportunities:
  - Use broad match keywords and automatic campaigns to uncover new search terms that resonate with customers.

- Expand Long-Tail Keywords:
  - Identify long-tail variations of successful keywords to target niche audiences with higher purchase intent.

- Add Negative Keywords:
  - Exclude irrelevant or low-converting search terms using negative keywords to improve efficiency.

6. Testing and Experimentation

Continuous testing is key to improving campaign performance. Here are some elements you can test:

- Keyword Match Types:
  - Experiment with broad match, phrase match, and exact match keywords to see which deliver the best results for specific terms.

- Ad Copy and Creative:
  - Test different headlines or images (if applicable) in Sponsored Brand or Sponsored Display ads to find the most engaging content.

- Budget Allocation:
  - Shift budgets between campaigns or ad groups based on their performance. For example, allocate more budget to high-converting campaigns during peak seasons.

- Bid Strategies:
  - Test different bidding strategies (e.g., dynamic bids vs. fixed bids) to see which maximizes ROI.

7. Seasonal Adjustments

Seasonality can significantly impact customer behavior on Amazon. Monitor trends during peak periods like holidays or back-to-school season and adjust your campaigns accordingly:

- Increase budgets for high-demand periods.
- Add seasonal keywords (e.g., "Christmas gifts").
- Monitor ACoS closely during these times as competition may drive up CPCs.

8. Automating Campaign Optimization

Managing multiple campaigns manually can be time-consuming. Consider using automation tools to streamline the process:

- Tools like Helium 10, Sellics, or Jungle Scout offer features like automated bid adjustments and keyword optimization.

- Amazon's own Campaign Manager allows you to set rules for bid adjustments based on performance thresholds (e.g., increase bids for keywords with CTR above a certain percentage).

Automation ensures consistent monitoring and optimization without requiring constant manual intervention.

9. Avoiding Common Mistakes

Here are some pitfalls to avoid when monitoring and adjusting campaigns:

- Overreacting Too Quickly:
  - Allow sufficient time (at least two weeks) before making major adjustments based on performance data.

- Neglecting Underperforming Campaigns:
  - Don't focus solely on high-performing campaigns; analyze why other campaigns are underperforming and make necessary changes.

- Ignoring Incremental Changes:
  - Small adjustments over time often yield better results than drastic changes all at once.

10. Creating a Routine for Monitoring

To stay on top of your campaigns, establish a regular routine for monitoring performance:

1. Daily: Check impressions, clicks, and spend to ensure budgets aren't being depleted too quickly.
2. Weekly: Review Search Term Reports and adjust bids or add negative keywords as needed.
3. Monthly: Evaluate overall campaign performance metrics like ACoS and ROAS. Make larger strategic adjustments if necessary.

Conclusion

Monitoring and adjusting your Amazon Sponsored Ads campaigns is an ongoing process that requires attention to detail and data-driven decision-making. By tracking key metrics like CTR, conversion rates, and ACoS while refining bids and keyword targeting over time, you can ensure continuous improvement in campaign performance. In the next chapter, we'll explore real-world case studies that demonstrate how these strategies come together in successful advertising campaigns!

Chapter 7: Case Studies and Practical Applications

Understanding the theory behind Amazon Sponsored Ads is essential, but seeing these strategies in action can provide valuable insights into how they work in real-world scenarios. In this chapter, we'll explore case studies of successful campaigns and analyze the practical applications of keyword strategies, bid adjustments, and campaign optimization. These examples will help you better understand how to apply the concepts discussed in previous chapters to your own campaigns.

Case Study 1: Launching a New Book with Limited Data

Scenario:
An author is launching a new self-help book titled "Overcoming Anxiety for Beginners." Since this is their first book, they have no prior sales data or audience insights to guide their advertising strategy.

Challenges:
- Limited data on high-performing keywords.
- Tight budget for advertising.
- Need to build visibility and generate initial sales.

Solution:
1. Start with Automatic Campaigns:
   - The author launched an automatic campaign with a daily budget of $20 to allow Amazon's algorithm to identify relevant search terms.
   - After two weeks, they analyzed the Search Term Report to identify high-performing keywords such as "anxiety relief book" and "self-help guide for beginners."

2. Transition to Manual Campaigns:
   - The author created a manual campaign using the identified keywords, splitting them into ad groups by match type (broad, phrase, exact).
     - For example:
       - Broad Match: "anxiety relief book"
       - Phrase Match: "self-help guide for beginners"
       - Exact Match: "overcoming anxiety book"

3. Refine Targeting with Negative Keywords:
   - They added negative keywords like "free," "cheap," and "children's books" to avoid irrelevant clicks.

4. Monitor and Adjust:
   - By tracking metrics weekly, they increased bids on high-converting keywords like "anxiety relief book" while lowering bids on underperforming terms.

Results:
- Within the first month, the campaign generated 50 sales with an ACoS of 25%, which was within their profit margin.
- The author used the data from this campaign to refine their targeting further and optimize future ads.

Case Study 2: Competing in a Crowded Niche

Scenario:
A seller is promoting a cookbook titled "Quick and Easy Vegan Recipes," competing in the highly saturated vegan cookbook market.

Challenges:
- High competition driving up cost-per-click (CPC).

- Difficulty standing out among established brands.
- Need to balance visibility with profitability.

Solution:
1. Focus on Long-Tail Keywords:
 - Instead of targeting broad terms like "vegan cookbook," the seller used long-tail keywords such as:
   - "quick vegan recipes for beginners"
   - "easy vegan meal prep cookbook"
   - "vegan recipes under 30 minutes"
 - These long-tail keywords had lower competition and higher conversion potential.

2. Leverage Seasonal Trends:
 - During January (popular for New Year's resolutions), they added seasonal keywords like "vegan recipes for weight loss" and increased their daily budget by 20%.

3. Utilize Competitor Keywords:
 - They targeted competitor names like "Thug Kitchen cookbook" to attract shoppers searching for similar products.
 - They ensured their product listing highlighted unique selling points (e.g., faster recipes) to differentiate from competitors.

4. Optimize Product Listing for Conversions:
 - The seller updated their product title, description, and bullet points to include high-performing keywords discovered through their campaigns.
 - They also added professional images and customer reviews to build trust.

5. Monitor Placement Performance:
 - Using placement reports, they found that ads at the top of search results generated the highest conversions. They increased bids specifically for this placement.

Results:
- The campaign achieved a CTR of 3% (above average for the niche) and a conversion rate of 10%.
- By focusing on long-tail and seasonal keywords, they reduced ACoS from 40% to 20% over three months.

Case Study 3: Scaling an Established Book Series

Scenario:
An author with an established mystery series wanted to scale their advertising efforts to boost sales across all books in the series while keeping ACoS low.

Challenges:
- Managing multiple books with different target audiences.
- Balancing ad spend across new releases and older titles.
- Avoiding cannibalization between ads for similar books.

Solution:
1. Use Portfolio Campaigns for Organization:

- The author grouped campaigns into portfolios based on each book in the series. This allowed them to track performance by title while managing budgets efficiently.

2. Promote New Releases with Branded Keywords:
   - For their latest release, they targeted branded keywords like "[Author Name] mystery series" and "[Book Title] mystery novel."
   - This ensured loyal readers searching for their name or series could easily find the new book.

3. Cross-Promote Older Titles with Sponsored Brands Ads:
   - They created Sponsored Brands ads featuring multiple books from the series with a headline like "Discover [Author Name]'s Mystery Series."
   - These ads directed shoppers to a custom Amazon Store page showcasing all titles in the series.

4. Analyze Keyword Overlap Across Books:
   - Using Search Term Reports, they identified overlapping keywords generating clicks across multiple books (e.g., "cozy mystery novel").
   - They allocated higher bids to these shared keywords while ensuring each book's ad copy highlighted its unique elements.

5. Leverage Reviews in Ad Copy (Where Applicable):
   - For Sponsored Display ads, they included snippets from customer reviews (e.g., "Readers are calling it 'the best mystery of the year'") to build credibility and attract clicks.

6. Adjust Budgets Based on Performance Trends:
   - They allocated more budget toward newer titles with higher growth potential while maintaining smaller budgets for older books that still generated consistent sales.

Results:
- Overall sales across the series increased by 30% within six months.
- ACoS remained stable at 15%, even as ad spend scaled up.
- Sponsored Brands ads drove significant traffic to their Amazon Store page, resulting in cross-sales of older titles.

Practical Applications

From these case studies, several key takeaways emerge that you can apply to your own campaigns:

1. Start Small and Scale Gradually:
   - Begin with automatic campaigns or broad match keywords to gather data before transitioning into more refined strategies like manual campaigns or exact match targeting.

2. Focus on Long-Tail Keywords in Competitive Niches:
   - Long-tail keywords are often overlooked but can deliver high-conversion traffic at lower CPCs.

3. Leverage Seasonal Opportunities:
   - Adjust your campaigns during peak seasons or trends to capture increased demand.

4. Use Branded Keywords Strategically:
   - Protect your brand by bidding on your name or product titles, especially if you have an established audience or series.

5. Optimize Product Listings Alongside Ads:
   - Ensure your product pages are optimized with relevant keywords, compelling descriptions, professional images, and strong reviews to maximize conversions from ad traffic.

6. Monitor Performance Regularly and Adapt Quickly:
   - Use tools like Search Term Reports and Placement Reports to identify what's working—and what isn't—and adjust bids or budgets accordingly.

Conclusion

These real-world examples highlight how different strategies can be tailored to specific goals, whether it's launching a new product, competing in a crowded niche, or scaling an established brand. By applying these lessons—alongside regular monitoring and optimization—you can create effective Amazon Sponsored Ads campaigns that drive visibility, clicks, and ultimately sales. In the next chapter, we'll explore tools and resources that can help streamline your keyword management and campaign optimization efforts!

Chapter 8: Tools and Resources for Keyword Management

Managing Amazon Sponsored Ads campaigns effectively requires more than just strategy—it also demands the right tools and resources to streamline processes, uncover insights, and optimize performance. With the vast array of keyword research tools, analytics platforms, and automation software available today, advertisers can save time, reduce errors, and maximize their return on investment (ROI). In this chapter, we'll explore the best tools and resources for keyword management and campaign optimization, as well as tips for integrating them into your workflow.

1. Why Use Tools for Keyword Management?

While Amazon's Advertising Console provides essential features for running campaigns, third-party tools offer advanced functionalities that can give you a competitive edge. Here's why using these tools is beneficial:

- Efficiency: Save time by automating repetitive tasks like bid adjustments or keyword discovery.
- Data-Driven Insights: Access detailed analytics on search volume, competition levels, cost-per-click (CPC), and more.
- Keyword Discovery: Uncover profitable keywords that may not be immediately obvious.
- Optimization: Continuously refine campaigns with tools that analyze performance and suggest improvements.

2. Top Tools for Keyword Research

These tools are specifically designed to help you find high-performing keywords and refine your targeting:

- **Helium 10 (Magnet & Cerebro):**
  - Magnet: A keyword research tool that generates thousands of relevant keywords based on a seed term.
  - **Cerebro:** A reverse ASIN lookup tool that reveals which keywords competitors are ranking for.
  - Features include search volume data, relevancy scores, and competitive analysis.

- **Jungle Scout (Keyword Scout):**
  - Provides keyword suggestions with metrics like search volume, PPC costs, and seasonal trends.
  - Ideal for finding long-tail keywords and identifying niche opportunities.

- **AMZScout:**
  - Offers reverse ASIN lookup functionality to analyze competitor keywords.
  - Includes keyword tracking and performance monitoring features.

- **Sonar by Sellics:**
  - A free Amazon-specific keyword research tool that generates keyword suggestions based on customer search behavior.
  - Includes features like reverse ASIN lookup and search volume estimates.

3. Tools for Campaign Optimization

Once you've identified your keywords, these tools can help you optimize your campaigns:

- **Sellics:**
  - An all-in-one Amazon advertising platform that provides automated bid adjustments, campaign analytics, and profitability tracking.
  - Features include ACoS optimization and performance forecasting.

- **Zon.Tools:**
  - Automates campaign management tasks like bid adjustments, keyword harvesting, and adding negative keywords.
  - Uses AI algorithms to optimize campaigns based on performance data.

- **PPC Entourage:**
  - Focused on Amazon PPC management with features like keyword optimization, budget tracking, and negative keyword automation.
  - Includes tools for analyzing Search Term Reports to refine targeting.

- **Ad Badger:**
  - Specializes in automating bid adjustments and negative keyword management.
  - Provides insights into ACoS trends and helps reduce wasted ad spend.

4. Tools for Tracking Performance

Monitoring campaign performance is crucial for making data-driven decisions. These tools provide detailed reporting and analytics:

- Amazon Advertising Console:
  - The built-in platform offers essential metrics like impressions, CTR, conversion rates, ACoS, and ROAS (Return on Ad Spend).
  - Use Search Term Reports to identify high-performing keywords and irrelevant terms.

- Data Dive by Brandon Young:
  - An advanced tool for analyzing campaign performance across multiple metrics simultaneously.
  - Helps identify trends in keyword performance over time.

- SellerApp:
  - Combines keyword research with campaign analytics to provide a comprehensive view of ad performance.
  - Offers features like competitor analysis and profitability tracking.

5. Free Resources for Keyword Research

If you're working with a limited budget or just starting out, these free resources can still provide valuable insights:

- Amazon Autocomplete:
  - Use Amazon's search bar to generate keyword ideas based on customer queries. Simply type in a seed term and note the suggested phrases.

- Google Trends:
  - Analyze search trends over time to identify seasonal or emerging keywords relevant to your product or book.

- AnswerThePublic:
  - Generates questions and phrases related to a topic based on search engine data. Useful for discovering long-tail keywords or content ideas.

6. Automation Tools

Automation can save time and ensure consistent campaign management. These tools are ideal for scaling your efforts:

- Bulk Operations in Amazon Advertising Console:
  - Allows you to make mass changes to campaigns by uploading spreadsheets. Useful for managing large campaigns efficiently.

- **Bid Optimization Software (e.g., Ad Badger):**
  - Automatically adjusts bids based on performance thresholds (e.g., increasing bids for high-converting keywords).

- **Campaign Automation Platforms (e.g., Zon.Tools):**
  - Automates tasks like adding new keywords from Search Term Reports or pausing underperforming ads.

7. Tips for Choosing the Right Tools

With so many options available, selecting the right tools can feel overwhelming. Here are some tips to guide your decision:

1. Define Your Needs:
  - Are you focused on keyword discovery? Campaign optimization? Performance tracking? Choose a tool that aligns with your primary goals.

2. Consider Your Budget:
  - Many tools offer tiered pricing plans or free trials. Start with basic plans if you're new to advertising or have a limited budget.

3. Look for Integration Options:
  - Some tools integrate directly with Amazon's Advertising Console or other platforms you use (e.g., inventory management software).

4. Evaluate Ease of Use:
  - Choose tools with user-friendly interfaces that don't require extensive training or technical expertise.

5. Test Before Committing:
  - Take advantage of free trials or demos to ensure the tool meets your needs before purchasing.

8. Leveraging Resources Beyond Tools

In addition to software solutions, there are other resources that can enhance your understanding of Amazon advertising:

- **Amazon Seller University:**
  - Offers free video tutorials on how to use Amazon's advertising platform effectively.

- **Online Communities:**
  - Join forums like the Amazon Seller Central Community or Facebook groups dedicated to Amazon PPC strategies to learn from other sellers' experiences.

- **Books & Courses:**
  - Invest in books or online courses that focus on advanced Amazon advertising

techniques (e.g., those offered by industry experts like Brian Johnson or Liran Hirschkorn).

9. Building an Efficient Workflow

To maximize the value of these tools and resources, create an efficient workflow:

1. Start with keyword research using tools like Helium 10 or Jungle Scout.
2. Launch campaigns in Amazon Advertising Console using your researched keywords.
3. Monitor performance weekly using Search Term Reports or third-party analytics platforms.
4. Refine campaigns by adding high-performing keywords as exact matches and excluding irrelevant terms as negatives.
5. Automate repetitive tasks like bid adjustments using software solutions.
6. Revisit your strategy monthly to incorporate new insights or adapt to market changes.

10. Combining Tools with Strategy

While tools are invaluable for streamlining processes, they should complement—not replace—your strategic thinking. Use them as aids to gather data, uncover insights, and automate routine tasks while applying the principles of effective campaign management discussed in earlier chapters.

Conclusion

The right combination of tools and resources can significantly enhance your ability to manage keywords, optimize campaigns, and achieve better results with Amazon Sponsored Ads. Whether you're just starting out or scaling an established business, leveraging these solutions will save time while improving ROI. In the final chapter of this book, we'll summarize key takeaways from all chapters and provide actionable steps to implement everything you've learned!

www.ingramcontent.com/pod-product-compliance
Lightning Source LLC
Chambersburg PA
CBHW070958220526
45471CB00007B/3084